Beautiful BUCKS COUNTY

A Photography Celebration
Through Four Seasons

DEREK FELL

Derek Fell (signature)

Cedaridge Farm Press

Box 1, Gardenville, Pennsylvania 18926

2

CONTENTS

Opposite: *Summer foliage of a sugar maple at historic Cedaridge Farm, near Pipersville, casts cooling shade on a humid day. Sugar maples are a prime source of maple syrup, which can be extracted from the trees during a brief warming spell in early spring. (Fig. 3)*

Left: *A rocky stream descends a steep slope, creating a series of cascades near the campground in Tohickon Valley Park, above Point Pleasant. The park also has cabins to rent in secluded clearings that overlook the picturesque Tohickon Creek. (Fig. 4)*

4

INTRODUCTION

Opposite: *Sunset over the Stover-Myers Dam, from a narrow stone bridge that crosses Tohickon Creek along Dark Hollow Road. The dam diverts water along a mill race that once powered a sawmill built in 1800. The mill was in continuous operation until 1956, and is now preserved as a museum by the Bucks County Parks system. (Fig. 5)*

Below: *An early morning sunrise along a line of deciduous trees, seen from Stover Park Road, in Tinicum Township. (Fig. 6)*

I am happy to see a book that finally shows the exquisite beauty of Bucks County, and I am especially pleased that the book features the stimulating color photography of Bucks County resident, Derek Fell, whose work as a writer and photographer I have long admired.

Derek was born in England — a country with characteristics strongly resembling those of Bucks County. I was born here to a Bucks County farming family, but like Derek I have travelled widely, and there is no place I would rather live than the heart of Bucks.

As the owner of Peddler's Village community of country stores, I was delighted when Derek described it in one of his articles as a unique commercial endeavor that embellishes the landscape. I would hate to be responsible for anything that could be considered a blight on this beautiful section of Pennsylvania.

I thought I knew every inch of Bucks County, until seeing Derek's photography for this book. The images made me realize how much I have overlooked, and as I leaf the pages I see places I never knew existed; I feel impelled to find them on the accompanying map and investigate them immediately.

I hope the reader feels the same way, whether a long time resident or casual visitor, for the more we appreciate the ethereal beauty of our surroundings the more we are likely to see it preserved for future generations.

Earl Jamison
Peddler's Village, Lahaska

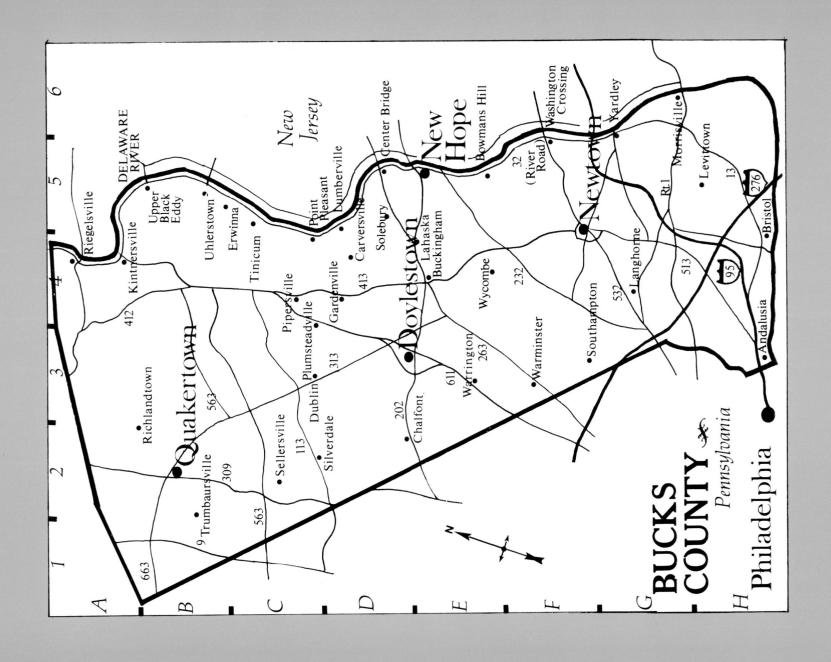

HISTORY

Bucks County, Pennsylvania is shaped like a boot with the toe touching the city of Philadelphia and the heel formed by a bend in the Delaware River. Named after Buckinghamshire, England, the birthplace of William Penn — founder of Pennsylvania — the county is famous for its spectacular natural beauty through all four seasons. Approximately 50 miles long by 25 miles wide, the county is blessed with gently rolling wooded hills threaded with rocky streams and fertile farms. It also features numerous large parks, several large recreational lakes, and the wild and scenic Delaware River

Below: *Each Christmas Day, a reenactment of General George Washington's crossing of the Delaware River, during the Revolutionary War, takes place at Washington Crossing State Park, watched by thousands of spectators who crowd both the Pennsylvania and New Jersey banks of the river. (Fig. 7)*

that forms its eastern boundary. Its principle towns are Newtown in the lower part of the county, Doylestown and New Hope in the central part and Quakertown in the upper part.

Though originally a prosperous agricultural area (and still largely agricultural), every kind of farming is represented, including dairy farms, poultry farms, tree farms, orchards, vineyards, vegetable farms and even fish farms. Its proximity to the large metropolitan areas of Philadelphia and New York City, however, have attracted residential development. These modern communities co-exist with historical buildings, such as water mills, old stagecoach taverns and stone farmhouses. Many famous people, including the impressionist painter, Edward Redfield; the songwriter, Oscar Hammerstein; and novelist, Pearl S. Buck, have owned property in the area. It is a wonderful place to live and an exciting place to visit.

The first people to settle Bucks County were the peaceful tribe of Lenni-Lenape Indians. They hunted game in its woodlands, fished its clear water streams, and cultivated crops such as corn and pumpkins in fertile plots, fenced to keep out foraging animals. Wolves and bears were abundant. The last wolf was killed near Pipersville in 1800 and bears occasionally still wander into Upper Bucks from the Pocono Mountains.

Left: At Pennsbury Manor, William Penn's country estate near Morrisville, on the north bank of the Delaware River, a life-size bronze statue of the founder of Pennsylvania, looks out toward the main house at the water's edge. (Fig. 8) Right: Pennsbury Manor house framed by an avenue of tall tulip trees at the edge of the Delaware River. (Fig. 9)

European settlement began in 1682 when William Penn arrived from England with a deed granting him considerable territory by King Charles II in payment of debts owed to Penn's father, a valiant admiral who had helped the King win victories in wars against the Dutch. Penn arrived with a shipload of Quaker followers seeking to form a self-sufficient colony free of religious persecution. Establishing Philadelphia as the capital city of his new state — named Pennsylvania (meaning "Penn's Woods" for the abundance of natural woodland) — Penn divided the territory into counties. He established in Bucks County, near Morrisville on the banks of the Delaware River, a model farm and country estate called Pennsbury Manor, requiring a five-hour barge ride upstream from Philadelphia. A restoration of Pennsbury Manor includes the main house, numerous outbuildings, orchards and gardens (see appendix for visiting hours).

William Penn always dealt fairly with the Indians, paying them for the purchase of land, and fostering their trust in the white settlers. This trust was broken in 1737 when Thomas Penn, Penn's son, enforced a "Walking Purchase" to ratify an old Indian deed of 1686 which granted lands to his family extending "a day and a half walk". Three specially chosen "run-

Left: *The Fonthill property, in Doylestown, is a romantic estate established by an eccentric archeologist, Dr. Henry C. Mercer. The buildings contain valuable collections of tiles, prints and engravings. (Fig. 10)* Right: *At his Fonthill estate Dr. Mercer established a Moravian Tile Works, which has been restored to working condition. (Fig. 11)*

ners'' started out at sunrise from Wrightstown, just north of Newtown; and one of them, Edward Marshall, reached a point 65 miles northwest by noon the following day. The Indians were infuriated by this trickery, and the incident was directly responsible for the Indians taking sides with the French in conflicts against the British before the Revolutionary War.

Historic Quakertown, Bucks County's largest community in Upper Bucks, is situated just north of Lake Nockamixon, a 5,253-acre park containing a man-made lake of more than 1,450 acres, created by damming the Tohickon Creek. The lake is large enough to allow power boating. Quakertown features an Historic District of old homes and antique stores. It was in Quakertown — at Liberty Hall — where America's symbol of freedom, ''The Liberty Bell,'' was hidden during the British occupation of Philadelphia.

During revolutionary times, New Hope was an important ferry crossing, but benefited immensely from the construction of the Delaware Division Canal in 1832. As many as 3,000 barges a year travelled from Bristol (Bucks County), to Easton (Northampton County). Until 1931, when a railroad provided faster transportation, mule-drawn barges carried coal and other products to Bristol, where the Delaware was navigable to Philadelphia and the open sea. Following its abandonment, the canal was declared a state park and dedicated a National Historic Landmark. Today the canal towpath is a favorite place to walk, fish and cycle. In the town of New Hope, visitors can board mule-drawn barges for a trip of eleven miles to Centre Bridge and return.

New Hope today is a haven for artists and writers, and its streets are thronged with tourists, especially on weekends during summer. The New Hope-Ivyland Railroad is a popular ride. A steam engine takes visitors across a wooden trestle bridge featured in the old silent movie *The Perils of Pauline* and on through some of the most scenic parts of Bucks County to the tiny station of Buckingham Valley and back.

The scenic, historic and cultural attractions of Bucks County are so many that residential development continues to be a major concern. However, conscious of the need to maintain an agricultural environment, a progressive plan has been adopted by the state and county to pay owners of large farms for development rights in order to preserve a rural landscape. Other incentives help to save historic buildings.

In 1888, shortly after the Civil War, Fordhook Farm was established in Doylestown as a research station for the Burpee Seed Company founded by a 16-year-old schoolboy, W. Atlee Burpee, with $1000 borrowed from his mother. Burpee quickly established the largest mail-order seed house in the world; and its Fordhook Farm produced many important hybrid varieties of flowers and vegetables, including the Fordhook lima bean, Big Boy tomato and Golden Bantam sweet corn.

Left: *Covered bridge opened to pedestrians only, spans a scenic section of Neshaminy Creek, in Tyler State Park, near Newtown. Comprising more than 1,700 acres it features some excellent riding, hiking and biking trails. (Fig. 12)* Right: *The Logan Inn, New Hope, is named for an Indian chief who took the name of James Logan, secretary to William Penn. (Fig. 13)*

The area of Bucks County around New Hope is especially famous for its antique stores. Hobensack & Keller specializes in garden furnishings, many of them imported from historic European estates. (Fig. 14)

In summer, special trains from Philadelphia would take visitors to see the test plots. After visiting Fordhook Farms in the early 1900's, the California plant wizard, Luther Burbank, wrote that Fordhook was the best of his Eastern object lessons and of value not only to Burpee's customers, but "to everyone who cultivates the earth".

The founder's son, David Burpee, took over from his father and was president for 50 years. Though the company still maintains its headquarters in nearby Warminster, historic Fordhook Farm is now a bed-and-breakfast inn run by Burpee family members.

Adjacent to Fordhook Farm is Delaware Valley College of Science and Agriculture, a farm school originally founded by Dr. Joseph Krauskopf to introduce Jewish boys to farming in North America. In spring, hundreds of acres of orchards surrounding the arboretum-like campus, burst into flower, followed by bountiful harvests of peaches, apples, pears, nectarines, grapes, plums and berry fruits.

Another enterprising venture nearby in Doylestown is a tile works established by Dr. Henry Chapman Mercer. Wealthy from inherited money, Dr. Mercer was fascinated with archeology, the supernatural, and the world of Dickens. He built several imposing structures in Doylestown, including a sinister mansion made entirely of cement, a castle-like museum to house a collection of tools depicting the history of commerce in America, and a Moravian tile works. After his death, the museum and house came under the care of the Bucks County Historical Society. Mercer's tiles have since been recognized as works of art, and the tile works — administered by the Bucks County Parks Department — still operates the facility, supplying an increasing demand for the product.

Following World War II, Bucks County saw the influx of many new industries and people. U.S. Steel established a large plant near Pennsbury Manor, with many of its employees housed in an immense residential development, called Levittown, in Lower Bucks.

Doylestown, the county seat, is centrally located, and an interesting town to explore for its old houses and predominantly Victorian architecture. To the north of town lies a beautiful 1,500 acre park, Peace Valley, which includes Lake Galena, a man-made lake, where sailing and fishing is popular. On a hill above the park is the Shrine of Czestochowa, a cathedral-like structure built mostly from donations by people of Polish ancestry as a memorial and national shrine.

Newtown is located just northeast of Levittown. It was the county seat before Doylestown. Newtown's streets were laid out by William Penn, and it still maintains an old world charm in the architecture of its 18th and 19th century buildings. The Newtown Historic District occupies the entire center of town — all of its houses listed on the National Historic Register. Newtown's most famous resident was Edward Hicks, the folk-art painter. Many of his important paintings, such as *The Peaceable Kingdom,* depict landscapes and farms in the vicinity. In the nearby community of Churchville, at the nature center, the first Saturday in October, Newtown's agricultural heritage is still recognized by the Giant Pumpkin Contest which attracts contestants from as far away as Texas.

Canada geese and mallard ducks congregate at a bend in the Tohickon Creek at Ralph Stover State Park, near Point Pleasant. The creek is stocked with trout each spring, and cabins can be rented close to a swimming hole popular with children. (Fig. 15)

Within a hundred years of William Penn's death, America was at war with England seeking independence. General George Washington commanded a ragtag revolutionary army and conducted parts of his campaign in Bucks County, especially along the Delaware River. In the winter of 1776, the river separated the two armies — the British camped in Trenton, New Jersey, and the American troops camped near Bowman's Hill, just south of New Hope.

Desperately in need of a victory, following a series of defeats, Washington decided to cross the Delaware at McConkey's Ferry (now called Washington's Crossing) and launch an attack. At nightfall on Christmas Day, in a bitterly cold blinding snowstorm, Washington crossed the ice-choked river in Durham boats. He marched to Trenton while the British forces were engaged in Christmas festivities, and in a surprise offensive achieved his first decisive victory of the war. This boosted American morale and spurred the Continental army to eventually win the war. The event is now celebrated each Christmas Day with a reenactment in authentic period costumes at Washington Crossing Historic Park. The park today includes a modern historical building featuring artifacts and a copy of the massive painting by Emmanuel Leutze showing George

Left: *The farmhouse of Burgess Lea was established in the 1700's, seen here from the River Road north of New Hope, across a field of sunflowers. (Fig. 16)*
Right: *Fordhook Farm, Doylestown — the home of the late David Burpee, dean of American seedsmen — is now a comfortable bed-and-breakfast inn. (Fig. 17)*

Washington crossing the frozen Delaware. A community of old homesteads, ferryman's house, and boathouse are also part of the park.

Further upriver, at Thompson's Mill, in the shadow of Bowman's Hill is another section of Washington Crossing Historic Park, including a graveyard of revolutionary soldiers and the Thompson-Neely House where Major General Lord Sterling and other officers planned battle strategy. The hill adjacent to the house rises 380 feet and today is topped by a 110 foot stone observation tower on a site that served Washington as a signal station. In the valley below sparkles Pidcock Creek which winds through the Bowman's Hill Wildflower Preserve before entering the Delaware River.

During the Revolutionary period, the area around nearby Buckingham and Tinicum was the domain of a band of four outlaws known as the Doan Brothers. Following a string of robberies, the brothers were tracked down by a group of vigilantes and cornered in a cabin near their home on the banks of the Tohickon Creek, above Point Pleasant.

Buckingham Mountain is rich in wildflowers and has a rock formation known as Wolf Rocks; where in 1858, a recluse named Albert Large lived alone in a cave for 20 years. Discovered by quarrymen, he became a national celebrity known as "the Hermit of Buckingham Mountain" and lived out his later years on a nearby farm.

Left: *Red covered bridge and yellow canal house that once served canal barges using the Delaware Canal, is part of the community of Uhlerstown. (Fig. 18)*

SPRING

Spring comes to Bucks County slowly at first, as winter seems reluctant to release its grasp on the land. Snowfalls have been known as late as early April and light frosts can still chill the garden in early May. Alternating cold spells and warm spells energize sleeping buds into bloom, first evident with red maple flowers that tint the treetops with a ruddy glow, while underneath transluscent green lettuce-like leaves of skunk cabbage strike through the snow, even ahead of the dazzling golden-yellow forsythia and daffodil displays.

Bowman's Hill Wildflower Preserve, just south of New Hope, off the River Road, is a beautiful place to observe the miracle of spring. Coursed by the sparkling clear waters of Pidcock Creek, the preserve has natural stands of spire-like red cedars, billowing white pines and lofty Canadian hemlock, mingling their dark green hues with the lighter mint-green freshness of unfurling leaves from native deciduous trees — notably rock-steady sugar maples, towering tulip trees and graceful dogwoods.

Rustic trails meander through numerous wildflower habitats that reach peak bloom in early May. White

Right: *Trees edging a farm pond in Solebury Township, project brilliant shafts of sunlight as the sun rises on a humid spring day. (Fig. 19)*

bloodroot anemones, nodding Virginia bluebells and colonies of celandine poppies are just a small sampling of brightly colored plants that emerge from dormancy to flower and set seed even before the trees are in full leaf.

Rocky streams sparkle from the release of abundant ground moisture and silvery shad — a salmon-like fish — begins its annual migration from the ocean up the Delaware River to its spawning grounds in the Pocono Mountains and beyond. Stocked with trout by the state, the picturesque Tohickon Creek becomes a Mecca for fishermen, especially the section between Stover Park and Myer's Dam, at the border of Plumstead and Tinicum townships.

In New Hope mule barge rides begin along the Delaware Canal towpath, taking visitors on a smooth, relaxing ride for one to several hours duration. Paralleling the scenic Delaware River, the canal's banks are arched over with stout buttonwood trees; between them can be seen quaint cottages and artists' studios.

Left: *The Golden Pheasant Restaurant, on the River Road at Erwinna, features a dining room in a greenhouse setting. (Fig. 20)*

Right: *Lentenboden Bulb Garden, on the River Road, north of New Hope, features thousands of tulips, daffodils and other spring-flowering bulbs from mid-April through mid-May. (Fig. 21)*

Farmers throughout the county till their land to plant mostly cereal grains, corn and soy beans, often discing ribbons of fertile soil in wide sweeps up tree-fringed slopes, creating beautiful patterns as they contour the land for erosion control. The Delaware Valley College of Science and Agriculture, outside Doylestown, stages an Agricultural Day in April, featuring livestock judging and numerous demonstrations connected with Bucks County's rich farming heritage.

The Strawberry Festival at Peddler's Village, Lahaska, draws visitors from as far as Washington, D.C. and New York for an opportunity to sample strawberry products (such as chocolate-covered strawberries) at more than 60 country stores and outdoor vendor's stalls that also feature local crafts. The first week of June marks the start of the local strawberry season when many U-pick farms offer juicy sun-ripened strawberries at bargain prices.

Tranquil woodland along Cabin Run Creek, near Pipersville, sparkles bright green from freshly un-furled leaves. This area is owned by the Bucks County Nature Conservancy. (Fig. 22)

Pink-flowering dogwoods seem to light up the sky along Cafferty Road, above Point Pleasant, near the Tohickon Valley Park. The pink is a mutation from the white-flowering dogwood that grows wild along hedgerows and waysides of Bucks County, its flowering signifying the height of spring. (Fig. 23)

Seven-year-old Vicki Fell seems dwarfed by a large cave extending into a cliff face near High Rocks State Park. Legend has it that in a cave like this the Doan Outlaw gang hid a strong box with treasure stolen in the mid-1700's. (Fig. 24)

Rock climber negotiates a sheer rock wall along precipitous cliffs at High Rocks State Park, off Cafferty Road, Point Pleasant. Hiking trails along the cliff tops lead to scenic overlooks with spectacular views of the Tohickon Valley. (Fig. 25)

25

View from the front porch of Andalusia, an historic 19th century Greek revival manor house on the north bank of the Delaware River, built for a prominent Philadelphia family, Mr. and Mrs. John Craig. Their daughter Jane married Nicholas Biddle, a prominent banker who engaged in an historic confrontation with President Andrew Jackson over the control of the nation's currency. The grounds include beautiful rose gardens and perennial borders. (Fig. 26)

Quaint Victorian-style house with a picket fence and pink flowering rhododendron, typifies homes along the River Road, especially at Point Pleasant and Lumberville — riverside villages favored as weekend retreats by many writers and artists. (Fig. 27)

Bridge across the Delaware Canal at Nockamixon Palisades — a section of high cliffs along the River Road, near Kintnersville, in the northern section of Bucks County. The entire length of the Delaware Canal is part of the Theodore Roosevelt State Park, enjoyed by picnickers, walkers and bicyclists. (Fig. 28)

Right: *A secluded waterfall — within sight of the River Road at Point Pleasant — tumbles down a steep, rocky slope toward the Delaware River. A much higher waterfall can be seen at Ringing Rocks, a 64-acre county park two miles west of Upper Black Eddy. (Fig. 29)*

SUMMER

Summer in Bucks County is a paradise for those who enjoy the thrill of adventure sports or the tranquility of a scenic hike or secluded picnic. Days are usually warm and sunny, and nights pleasantly cool — except for a period around midsummer when the heat and humidity may persist into the night, with intermittent relief from occasional thunderstorms.

Tubing on the Delaware is a favorite way to cool off. Tube rentals are available in Point Pleasant, on the River Road, above New Hope, where buses transport tubes and tubers to Upper Black Eddy, Reigelsville, and even farther upriver, where boat ramps permit safe and easy access to the wide river. Its smooth, gently flowing current allows tubers to float lazily back to Point Pleasant, with the excitement of several shallow white-water rapids to negotiate.

Boating on Lake Galena, at Peace Valley Park, north of Doylestown, and also at Lake Nockamixon, between Dublin and Quakertown, are both popular places to seek relief from summer's heat. Canoeing, sailing and windsurfing are popular at Lake Galena, while power-boating is permitted on the larger Lake Nockamixon,

Left: *This magnificent white oak in a field opposite the Thompson-Neely Church, in the shadow of Bowman's Tower, is located in a field off the River Road, south of New Hope. (Fig. 30)* Right: *Vicki and Derek Fell Jr. eagerly explore a field of wild sunflowers. (Fig. 31)*

which also features a modern swimming pool.

Many communities stage summer theater productions by amateurs, notably Town & Country Players, in Buckingham, while the New Hope Playhouse Theater features professional performances.

The Doylestown Farmers Market in the center of town offers fresh, local grown produce every Saturday. Organically-grown fruits and vegetables — plus delicious home-baked breads and colorful, fragrant cut flowers — sell out quickly, so get there before noon. At Rice's Auction, near Lahaska, a larger market is open for business every Tuesday morning, drawing merchants and customers from a wider area.

The Fourth of July is celebrated with fireworks displays in many communities, and several museums offer interesting exhibits of not only the Revolutionary War period, but also Bucks County's industrial and agricultural past. Sunday afternoons provide excellent demonstrations and house tours at Pennsbury Manor, the country home of William Penn, founder of Pennsylvania; Washington Crossing State Park features Colonial houses and a modern museum complex with artifacts of the Revolutionary War; the Country Store Museum, in Quakertown, features products from a

Left: *A sheep peaks out from a moss-covered animal shelter beneath massive buttonwood trees along Cuttalossa Road, near Centre Bridge. The Cuttalossa Creek, overhung with wild rhododendrons along its entire length, flows behind the shelter. (Fig. 32)*
Right: *Sheep pasture along the Cuttalossa Road. (Fig. 33)*

bygone age. Perhaps the most well-preserved links to the past can be seen by visiting The Mercer Mile, in Doylestown, where Dr. Henry Mercer — an archaeologist — created a sinister castle-like structure as his home, a Moravian tileworks that is still in operation and a museum to display his incredible collection of tools representing the industry of man. All three buildings have a supernatural aura, and leave visitors awed at the energy and creativity of this extraordinary individual who never married, left no heirs, but established a valuable enduring legacy for all the world to enjoy.

Summer is a good time to consider a balloon ride above Bucks County. Rides start most days at Lahaska and Pipersville, balloonists taking participants for an exhilarating ride high over the Delaware River into New Jersey.

August finds New Hope a hive of activity for its annual Auto Show, at the Solebury High School, while the Memorial Field in Doylestown, stages an Outdoor Antique Show, where many of the area's dealers exhibit their choicest pieces.

Left: *Garden shed framed by hollyhocks is a landscape feature at the home of Earl Jamison, owner of the Peddler's Village community of country stores. The farm is located in Solebury Township. (Fig. 34)*

Right: *Cutting garden at Cedaridge Farm, Tinicum Township, features a Victorian-style gazebo. (Fig. 35)*

Private home in New Hope features a balcony with a view of the Delaware River. The balcony is festooned with climbing roses and beds of perennials, including yellow loosestrife. (Fig. 36)

Colorful beds of impatiens and other flowering annuals are a summer-long feature of Peddler's Village, a community of country stores in Lahaska. (Fig. 37)

Left: *Stover Farm, Buckingham Township, across a field of soy beans. The farm also grows tomatoes in greenhouses during winter, melons and sweet corn during summer, sold from a farm stand on the property. (Fig. 38)*

Right: *Bountiful vegetable garden at Cedaridge Farm, Tinicum Township, uses only organic methods. Herds of foraging deer — the biggest problem to a productive garden in many areas of Bucks County — are fenced out. (Fig. 39)*

Left: *The post office of Gardenville was named after this beautiful flower garden located opposite the Gardenville Hotel, and a short walk from the post office. The pink cosmos reseed themselves every year. (Fig. 40)*

Right: *Floral arrangements displayed at Cedaridge Farm, Tinicum, with an old stone springhouse in the background. Cedaridge Farm — like many old farm properties in Bucks County — is used as a location for catalog and magazine photography. (Fig. 41)*

Left: *Bowman's Hill Tower, in high summer, framed by leafy branches and vines that surround Bowman's Hill Wildflower Preserve south of New Hope. On an adjacent property is the Thompson-Neely "House of Decision" where General George Washington's commanders plotted Revolutionary War strategy. (Fig. 42)*

Right: *View of the Tohickon Creek in autumn colors from a scenic overlook at High Rocks State Park, adjoining Ralph Stover State Park, in Tinicum Township. For a similar view in spring, see page 1. (Fig. 43)*

AUTUMN

There is no need to travel into Vermont to see spectacular fall color. The changing color of leaves in Bucks County — especially at High Rocks above Point Pleasant, and all along the Delaware River, is as intense as anywhere in North America. Maples, hickories and tulip poplars in particular turn brilliant russet colors, lighting up the landscape. A leisurely walk or bicycle ride along the Delaware Canal towpath is a good way to see the colors. The High Rocks overlook — part of the Ralph Stover Park system — offers a breathtaking eagle's eye view of the Tohickon Valley. A miniature Grand Canyon, the view in all directions is spellbinding, with walking trails leading along the cliff top and down to the creek below. The sheer cliff faces at High Rocks attract groups of rock climbers who negotiate sheer drops and rock overhangs with rock climbing equipment.

The Tohickon Creek that runs below High Rocks into the Delaware River, at Point Pleasant, draws other thrill-seekers the first weekend in November when white-water enthusiasts (kayakers, rafters and canoers) take advantage of high water along the Tohickon to negotiate a string of surging rapids produced by excess water released from a dam at Lake Nockamixon. The most thrilling section begins at Ralph Stover State Park and snakes for six miles among boulder-strewn steeply wooded slopes to its confluence with the Delaware River.

Another good way to see the fall leaf colors is by taking a ride by steam train from the railroad station in New Hope to Buckingham Valley — a distance of 9 miles through some of Bucks County's most beautiful countryside. The 90-minute ride provides a spectacular view of Buckingham Mountain's wooded slopes on one side and open farmland on the other.

Numerous farm stands feature pies and preserves made from local fruit farms, and displays of plump pumpkins harvested locally. Churchville Nature Center stages a Giant Pumpkin Contest where local growers compete for cash prizes, some pumpkins weighing over 600 lbs.! The last local-grown peaches and sugar-sweet sweet corn can also be purchased for fresh eating (look for the late-ripening Iron Mountain peach — a local favorite with chin-dripping sweetness).

Left: *Old stone springhouse at Cedaridge Farm, near Pipersville, helped to keep perishable foods — such as milk and eggs — fresh for extended periods. The structure contains a flagstone trough with running water where fish could be kept alive for several weeks. (Fig. 44)*

Right: *The entrance to Cedaridge Farm, near Pipersville, during late fall when leaves from sugar maples and Japanese maples are allowed to carpet the ground, before being swept up and collected into bins. The leaves rot down and create leaf mold — a valuable soil conditioner for flower beds and vegetable plots. (Fig. 45)*

Craft Festivals draw crowds to the Grange Fairgrounds, Wrightstown, and also Tyler State Park, Newtown, while quilt enthusiasts can marvel over exhibits at Milford Middle School, Quakertown, and the Mercer Museum, Doylestown.

The cavernous Mercer Museum is also host to an event called The Savory Sampler — a fund raiser that allows donors to sample gourmet food from various area restaurants, with live music and dancing into the late hours.

For children and the young at heart, the annual Scarecrow Contest at the Peddler's Village community of country stores, guaranteed to raise a smile and a laugh at the ingenuity of entrants. Peddler's Village ends the fall season with a popular Apple Festival, featuring crafts and fresh cider pressed on the spot from apples grown in local orchards.

September is crammed with events, including the Polish Festival at the Shrine of Czestochowa, north of Doylestown, and the Scottish Festival, at the County Police Athletic Grounds, in Pipersville.

At the Peace Valley Winery above Lake Galena, visitors can pick delicious dessert-quality grapes for fresh eating right off the vine, or purchase award-winning wines. Buckingham Valley Vineyards, Buckingham, Bucks Country Vineyards, Aquetong, and Sandhill Winery, Erwinna, also offer local-grown wines of excellent quality from local-grown grapes.

Colonial-style cabins along Cuttalossa Road, near Centre Bridge, serve as animal shelters. The large native buttonwood tree in the rear overhangs Cuttalossa Creek, which rises about a mile distant from several springs and empties nearby into the Delaware River over a spectacular waterfall at the Cuttalossa Inn. (Fig. 46)

A series of ponds, fed by a spring, descend a slope in the garden of Earl Jamison, owner of the Peddler's Village community of country stores. This water course, located in Solebury Township, resembles a similar landscape feature in the center of the village. (Fig. 47)

Decorative barn door in Solebury Township features a hooded overhang with a heart cut-out similar to decorations found on Amish and Mennonite farms in nearby Lancaster County. A rambling grape vine exhibits beautiful autumn hues. (Fig. 48)

A colorful traditional scarecrow entered in the Peddler's Village annual Scarecrow Contest, which awards prizes to different categories of creative effort. The scarecrows are displayed around the village green, in the center of Peddler's Village in late September. (Fig. 49)

Phillips Mill Inn, romantic restaurant on the River Road just north of New Hope, decorates the entrance for Thanksgiving with a wreath of ornamental grasses and hanging baskets planted with ornamental kale. (Fig. 50)

Left: *A panorama of deciduous trees and evergreens at the height of fall coloring, seen from the railroad tracks which cross Street Road at the division of Solebury and Buckingham Townships. (Fig. 51)*

Majestic sugar maple, almost bare of leaves, shows a handsome silhouette of outstretched branches at Cedaridge Farm, near Pipersville. The sugar maple has extremely hard wood, and is a source of sap used for making maple syrup. (Fig. 52)

Maples on a street in Doylestown, brilliant with fall colors, not only light up the sky but create a rich carpet of rustic hues. (Fig. 53)

Right: *Water-powered mill at Bowman's Hill Wildflower Preserve, south of New Hope, used to take its power from the nearby Pidcock Creek by means of a mill-race. Foreground is jeweled with native New England asters. (Fig. 55)*

Right: *The annual Churchville Giant Pumpkin Contest draws contestants from Pennsylvania, New Jersey, and even Texas. Here, a local newspaper reporter makes a note of contestants' names and addresses prior to the weighing ceremony. Weights exceeding 600 lbs. have been recorded. The event is staged at the Churchville Nature Center, a 172-acre preserve in early October. (Fig. 54)*

WINTER ～

now can fall in Bucks County as early as the first week in October, but usually the ground does not freeze until after Christmas. Snowfalls can be light — tinting the landscape like icing sugar — or heavy — transforming the landscape into a collage of Christmas card scenes.

Drive the River Road to see ice formations along the towering cliff faces that begin above Lumberville. Portions of the Delaware Canal often make excellent skating, also the Duck Pond in the center of Yardley, and Lake Galena, in Peace Valley Park, where ice fishermen also try their luck. Some of the parks encourage cross-country skiing along groomed trails, and deer hunting season finds the fields and woods filled with eager hunters.

After Thanksgiving festivities, Christmas becomes the main focus. The downtown areas of Newtown, Doylestown, New Hope and Quakertown are decorated with Christmas lights and nativity scenes. They are all good places to shop for gifts. At the Peddler's Village

Left: *Cradle Valley Farm, Solebury Township, is a splendid example of many stone farmhouses established by Quaker farming families throughout Bucks County. (Fig. 56)*

Right: *Maples and ash trees arch over Pidcock Creek, in Buckingham Township, creating a cathedral effect on a wintry morning. (Fig. 57)*

community of country stores shoppers will not only enjoy a festival of Christmas lights but also a display of creative gingerbread houses.

Candlelight services are held at many area churches, and at Washington Crossing there is a patriotic re-enactment on Christmas Day of George Washington crossing the Delaware River, which resulted in the victorious Battle of Trenton.

The Pearl S. Buck home, near Perkasie, is just one of many historic places that puts on Christmas festivities. Furnished with lovely Oriental and American art, collected by the famous novelist, the Christmas house tour is fascinating. Contrast this with a visit to Pennsbury Manor, near Morrisville, during their Holly Night festivities and house tour.

Many of Bucks County's old stagecoach inns and taverns create an especially romantic atmosphere at Christmas, with beautiful holiday wreaths, dried floral arrangements, roaring log fires, candlelight suppers and piano music. Some offer sensational Sunday brunches with all you can eat at an economical fixed price.

Left: *Exquisite stonework characterizes many water-powered mills throughout Bucks County. The Stover-Myer sawmill on Dark Hollow Road, near Pipersville, was a working mill into the 1930's. Today it serves as a museum. (Fig. 58)*

Right: *Spectacular waterfall on the grounds of Cuttalossa Inn, near Centre Bridge, is within view of the River Road. During the tourist season, diners can eat outdoors on terraces that provide a magnificent view of the waterfall. (Fig. 59)*

Winter is a good time to browse the area's antique stores and art galleries. The impressionist oil paintings of Edward Redfield and the watercolors of Ranulph Bye show scenes of beautiful Bucks County landscapes, and are highly valued.

Charming bed-and-breakfast inns have been established throughout the county, offering cozy rooms with fireplaces and four-poster beds. A famous advertisement for a lodging along the River Road exclaims: "If you can't be a house guest in Bucks County, be ours!" That brilliant piece of salesmanship seems to sum up the spirit of Bucks County — a great place to live and a great place to visit!

An old stone farmhouse stands deserted along the banks of Cabin Run Creek, Plumstead Township. Local residents believe that the Doan Outlaws — a band of robber brothers — lived here in the 1700's, when they terrorized Bucks County with a series of violent robberies. (Fig. 60)

Farmhouse and its cluster of outbuildings sit solidly on the crest of a hill in Tinicum Township where township supervisors work earnestly to maintain the agricultural heritage of an area that still prides itself on expansive vistas free from development. (Fig. 61)

Tohickon Valley in mid-winter, seen from a scenic overlook at High Rocks State Park, on Tory Road, Point Pleasant; the Tohickon Creek wanders among these rolling hills, most of it a boy scout camp or part of the Ralph Stover State Park. (Fig. 62)

An arched stone bridge spans Pidcock Creek in Buckingham Township, leading to the main house of an old farm estate. (Fig. 63)

61

Left: *The farmhouse at Cedaridge Farm, near Pipersville, has foundations that date to the 1790's. A signature stone near the property — heavily eroded and difficult to read — seems to be dated 1691. (Fig. 64)*

Above: *The distinctive peak-roofed railroad station at Wycombe village, Buckingham Township, is similar to one in New Hope. Both are part of scenic stretch of railroad known as the New Hope-Ivyland, connecting two Bucks County communities. (Fig. 65)*

Above: *A massive field of boulders covers a clearing in the woods at Ringing Rocks State Park, near Upper Black Eddy. Deposited here by a glacier during the last Ice Age, the huge boulders — some of them as big as elephants — contain metals that produce a bell-like ringing sound when struck with a hammer. (Fig. 66)*

Right: *Animal shelter coated with snow in a sheep pasture along the Cuttalossa Creek, Solebury Township. For a similar scene in spring, see page 32. (Fig. 67)*

Left: *Glistening ice formations along Cabin Run Creek, Plumstead Township. Similar ice formations, resembling frozen waterfalls, line the River Road north of Lumberville during freezing winter months. (Fig. 68)*

Right: *Walk bridge at Lumberville, on the River Road in Solebury Township. The stone supports used to carry a covered bridge and vehicles, but after the original span was swept away in a flood, the suspension walk bridge took its place. Walkers can take a leisurely stroll over the Delaware River to Bulls Island State Park on the Jersey side of the river. (Fig. 69)*

Left: *Stover-Myer Sawmill, near Pipersville, was once powered by a waterwheel. The structure today is maintained by the Bucks County Park System as a museum. (Fig. 70)*

Right: *Melting snows swell the Tohickon Creek on Dark Hollow Road, Tinicum Township, creating a dramatic flow of water over the spillway known as Myers Dam. See page 4 for a sunset reflected on the mirror-smooth surface of the dam during a normal flow. (Fig. 71)*

Bucks County State & County Parks

For a free guide or more information about state and county parks, contact the Bucks County Department of Parks and Recreation, 901 E. Bridgetown Pike, Langhorne, PA 19047.

Black Ditch, Bristol – 80 acres with baseball field and hiking.

Churchville Nature Center, Churchville – 172 acres of hiking trails.

Core Creek, Newtown – 1,185 acres with fishing, boating, camping.

Delaware River Access Area, Andalusia – 8 acres for fishing, boating.

Frosty Hollow, Middletown – 95 acres for hiking and picnicking.

High Rocks Park, Point Pleasant – 7 acres of scenic trails.

Lake Towhee, Applebachsville – 501 acres with fishing, boating, hiking.

Mercer Tile Works, Doylestown – 10 acres with historic exhibits.

Neshaminy Park, Croydon – 330 acres with swimming, boating, fishing.

Nockamixon Park, near Quakertown – 5,253 acres with swimming, boating, fishing.

Oxford Valley Park, Oxford Valley – 43 acres for swimming, fishing, hiking.

Peace Valley, Doylestown – 1,500 acres with fishing, boating, hiking.

Pennsbury Manor, Tullytown – 43 acres with picnicking and historic tours.

Playwicki, Langhorne – 33 acres for fishing and hiking.

Queen Anne, Middletown – 169 acres with baseball field and hiking trails.

Ralph Stover, Point Pleasant – 45 acres with fishing, boating, swimming.

Ringing Rocks, Upper Black Eddy – 65 acres with hiking trails.

Silver Lake, Bristol – 291 acres with fishing, boating, hiking.

Stover-Myers Mill, Pipersville – 21 acres with picnicking and exhibits.

Tamanend Park, Richboro – 104 acres with hiking trails.

Theodore Roosevelt State Park, Delaware River – 60 acres for hiking.

Tinicum Park, Erwinna – 126 acres mostly for picnicking.

Tohickon Valley, Point Pleasant – 536 acres with fishing, swimming, hiking.

Tyler State Park, Newtown – 1,711 acres with fishing, boating, hiking.

Washington Crossing Park, New Hope & Washington Crossing – 500 acres for mostly hiking and exhibits.

Weisel Youth Hostel, near Quakertown – 8 acres with fishing and hiking.

Left: *Paunacussing Creek, seen from a stone bridge crossing Sawmill Road, just outside the village of Carversville, ablaze with the colors of a Bucks County fall. (Fig. 72)*

Right: *Cabin Run Creek, Plumstead Township, cascades over ruler-straight rock shelves that once produced brick-shaped stones valued by early settlers for building stone cabins and farmhouses. (Fig. 73)*

CONCLUSION

To me Bucks County is not just a pretty place to live or visit as a tourist. It has a power that seems to make you feel at peace. As a writer and photographer on travel and gardens I have visited many scenic areas of North America, including the rugged Big Sur coastline of California, the verdant alpine meadows of Mount Rainier, Washington state, and the magnificent Sonora Desert near Tucson, Arizona, but none of these places has impressed me so much as the serenity of Bucks County through all four seasons.

Not only am I awed by the natural beauty of Bucks County — especially the towering Palisades cliffs of Nockamixon Township and the glittering rushing waters of the boulder-strewn Tohickon Creek, but also the man-made beauty that abounds. The old stagecoach taverns are wonderful places to pause for refreshment, and the Delaware Canal towpath, one of the finest hiking and jogging trails I have ever experienced. I also admire the many farms that create such beautiful clear vistas across the rolling terrain.

I hope this book will make people more acutely aware of the paradise that is Bucks County, and instill the same kind of passion I feel for living here and capturing its many moods on film.

Derek Fell
Cedaridge Farm, Tinicum

Front of the Carversville General Store, in Solebury Township. A picturesque village of mostly stone and clapboard houses, the entire village is designated a historic district. Fleecydale Road, a twisting, winding road from Carversville to Lumberville, follows the Paunacussing Creek, and is considered one of the most scenic country roads in Bucks County. (Fig. 74)

70

PLACES OF INTEREST

Andalusia, a National Historic Landmark, the house is believed to be the nation's finest example of 19th century Greek Revival architecture. The elaborate shrub, rose and perennial gardens are also superb. Call (215) 848-1777 for appointment and directions.

Bristol Riverside Theater, Radcliffe and Market Streets, Bristol. Amateur groups stage live performances on the north bank of the Delaware during the summer season. Info: (215) 788-7827.

Bucks County Playhouse, 70 South Main Street, New Hope. The playhouse stages popular professional, theater productions during the tourist season. Info: (215) 862-2041.

Bucks County River Tubing, Pt. Pleasant. Buses transport you and rented tubes several miles up the Delaware River. You float back to base on the gentle current, involving a 3-4 hour trip. For a more adventurous ride, consider a 6-mile raft trip on the rugged Tohickon Creek, with white water and rapids along its entire length, at specified dates in spring and fall when conditions allow. Info: (215) 297-8181.

Coryell's Ferry Sightseeing Boat Rides
South Main Street, New Hope.
Pontoon boats, departing from behind Gerenser's Ice Cream Store, ply the Delaware River, providing passengers with a scenic river's-eye view of New Hope and Lambertville, on the New Jersey side. Info: (215) 862-2050.

David Library, Washington Crossing.
Original manuscripts and large reference collection devoted to research on the American Revolution.

Delaware Valley College's A-Day Fair, Doylestown.
The College holds its annual A-Day (Agricultural Day) in April. One of the few private agricultural schools in the nation DVC evokes the atmosphere of a state fair to its A-Day event.

Doylestown Farmer's Market
Municipal Parking Lot adjacent to Doylestown Inn, Doylestown.
Fresh fruits, vegetables, potted plants, cut flowers, and baked goods are offered every Saturday morning throughout the growing season.

Historic Fallsington, Fallsington.
Tour historic buildings, including stagecoach tavern and log house of colonial times. Info: (215) 295-6567.

Historic Newtown, Newtown.
Tour historic buildings listed in the National Register of Historic Places. Info: (215) 968-4004 or 968-2109.

James A. Michener Arts Center of Bucks County, Doylestown.
This museum exhibits American paintings and sculpture with special focus on major collections of Bucks County. Info: (215) 340-9800.

Keystone State Balloon Tours, Pipersville.
Champagne flights above beautiful Bucks countryside and across the majestic Delaware River, during the tourist season. Info: (215) 294-8034.

Mercer Folk Fest, Green Street, Doylestown.
During the second weekend in May, local artisans demonstrate their 18th and 19th century crafts at the annual Folk Fest held on the

grounds of Mercer Museum. Among the crafts demonstrated are woodcarving, tinsmithing, basketmaking, scherenschnitte, blacksmithing, coopering, folk art, and more. The festival includes militia drills, sheep shearing, quilting bee, and wagon rides, folk music and dancing. Country cooking and a number of other edibles are offered.

Mercer Museum, Fonthill, & The Moravian Tile Works, Doylestown.
Mercer Museum shows the growth and history of America through crafts. Info: (215) 345-0210.
Fonthill Museum displays tiles and prints from all over the world. Info: (215) 348-9461.
The craft of making the tiles can be viewed at The Moravian Tile Works. Info: (215) 345-6722.

Mule Barge Rides, South Main Street, New Hope.
Excursions of one, two, and three hours duration can be booked along the historic Delaware Canal. Info: (215) 862-2842.

National Shrine of Our Lady of Czestochowa
Ferry Road, Doylestown.
A Polish shrine (pronounced Chest-ah-hova) celebrating the culture and history of Poland. Info: (215) 345-0600.

Neshaminy State Park Theater, Bensalem.
Four comedies are performed from September through May. Info: (215) 673-5923 or 245-9487.

New Hope Steam and Railway Museum, New Hope.
Take a scenic 90 minute ride by steam train for 9 miles across a trestle bridge, through woodland, across prime farmland, and along the base of Buckingham Mountain to the railroad station of Buckingham Valley. Info: (215) 794-7188.

Parry Mansion, South Main Street, New Hope.
An 11-room, Georgian colonial mansion furnished in period styles of 1775 through 1900. Info: (215) 862-5652.

Pearl S. Buck Home, Perkasie.
Home of the author, the stone farmhouse is furnished with Oriental and American art. Info: (215) 249-0100.

Peddler's Village, Lahaska.
More than 60 country stores surrounding a village green and a number of good restaurants serving a wide range of foods to suit every budget.

Peddler's Village Dinner Theater, Cock 'n Bull Restaurant, Lahaska.
Country-style buffet plus musical, drama, and comedy performances. Info: (215) 794-3460.

Pennsbury Manor, Tullytown.
Restored country estate of the founder of Pennsylvania, William Penn. Special events staged year-round. Includes herb garden, orchards, mansion, and outbuildings. Info: (215) 946-0400.

Quarry Valley Farm, Street Road, Lahaska.
A working farm where children can pet animals, enjoy pony rides and special events. Info: (215) 794-5882.

Rice's Sale & Country Market, Green Hill Road, Lahaska.
A country market offering bargains galore, including fresh produce, crafts, clothing, and antiques. Every Tuesday before noon. Info: (215) 297-5993.

S.J. Gerenser Theater
Stockton Avenue & West Bridge Street, New Hope.

Cabin Run covered bridge, in Plumstead Township, spans Cabin Run Creek at its confluence with the wild and scenic Tohickon Creek. (Fig. 75)

Children's shows, dramas, musicals and comedies during the summer season. Info: (215) 862-3777.

Sesame Place, Oxford Valley Road, Langhorne.
Adventure theme park for children features numerous recreational attractions including flume rides into a swimming pool and characters from the famous hit children's television show, such as Big Bird. Info: (215) 757-1100 or 752-7070.

Summerseat, Morrisville.
Washington's headquarters briefly in winter, 1776. Later home of Robert Morris, signer of the Declaration of Independence. Info: (215) 295-7339.

Theater on the Towpath, 18-20 West Mechanic Street, New Hope.
Summer dinner theater offers French-style cuisine and a live show.

Town & Country Players, Old York Road, Buckingham.
A group of amateur performers stages several live theater shows during the summer. Info: (215) 348-7506.

Van Sant Airport, Headquarters Road, Erwinna.
Small airfield with grass runways. Participate in glider flights, bi-plane rides year-round. Info: (215) 847-8401.

VITA Garden Tour
A garden tour and brunch is held the first Sunday in June. Three Bucks County gardens are included on the tour which is for the benefit of VITA, Volunteers in Teaching Alternatives. For ticket information call (215) 345-8322 or 968-3484.

Vineyards
There are several to choose from, notably **Peace Valley Winery,** Old Limekiln Road, Chalfont; **Buckingham Valley Vineyards,** Route 413, Buckingham; **Bucks Country Vineyards,** Route 202, New Hope; and **Sand Castle Winery,** River Road, Erwinna.

Duck Pond in the center of Yardley is a favorite among skaters during winter freezes. The old section of Yardley features many historic buildings, antique stores and good restaurants. (Fig. 76)